Start Reading
AND **THINKING**

Dinosaur Explorer

Dougal Dixon

QEB Publishing

Published in the United States by
QEB Publishing, Inc.
23062 La Cadena Drive
Laguna Hills, CA 92653
www.qeb-publishing.com

Library of Congress Control Number 2005921259

ISBN 978-1-59566-533-1

Written by Dougal Dixon
Designed by Caroline Grimshaw
Editor Hannah Ray
Illustrated by Martin Knowelden

Series Consultant Anne Faundez
Publisher Steve Evans
Creative Director Louise Morley
Editorial Manager Jean Coppendale

Printed and bound in China

Contents

The world in the past

A long time ago, the world looked very different. The animals in those days were very different from today's animals.

Some of the strangest of these animals were the **dinosaurs**.

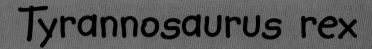

How big was
Tyrannosaurus rex?

Tyrannosaurus rex was the **fiercest** dinosaur of them all. It was larger than an elephant and was big enough to eat other dinosaurs.

You are lucky that you did not live in those days. Tyrannosaurus rex could have swallowed you whole!

Gallimimus

Gallimimus looked
a little like an ostrich.

It ran around the open
plains, eating insects
and small animals.

It used its long fingers
to dig in the ground
and look for food.

8

Gallimimus needed its long back legs to run away from fierce hunters like Tyrannosaurus rex.

How big was Gallimimus?

Diplodocus

Diplodocus was one of the biggest dinosaurs, but also one of the gentlest.

It was the size of a house and had a tiny head at the end of a long neck.

The main food of Diplodocus was leaves and twigs. It spent all its time eating to feed its enormous body.

How big was Diplodocus?

Ouranosaurus

Ouranosaurus was a big, plant-eating dinosaur. Its wide mouth helped it to eat plants from the ground.

Ouranosaurus had a brightly-colored **sail** on its back. It used this sail for **signaling** to other dinosaurs.

12

How big was
Ouranosaurus?

13

Stegosaurus

Stegosaurus had bony plates along its back. It also had spikes on the end of its tail that it used to fight off **enemies**.

Stegosaurus had a small head and a tiny **brain** the size of a walnut. Its jaws had small teeth for chewing up plants.

14

You would not have
been able to reach up to the
shoulder of Stegosaurus.

Triceratops

Three horns on the head of Triceratops made it look very fierce, like a rhinoceros.

It was a plant eater and used its horns to fight off meat eaters like Tyrannosaurus rex.

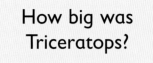

How big was
Triceratops?

Triceratops was one of
the last of the dinosaurs.

All dinosaurs are
now **extinct**.

17

Can you remember which was the fiercest dinosaur?

Which dinosaur was as big as a house?

18

Can you name two dinosaurs that start with the letter "T"?

Which dinosaur had a brightly-colored sail on its back?

Why did Gallimimus
need long legs?

Can you
remember
which dinosaur had
three horns on its head?

In every dinosaur,
which was longer—the
front or the back legs?

What does the word
"extinct" mean?

21

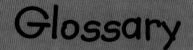

 **Brain**—the part of the head that people and animals use to think.

 **Dinosaur**—a type of animal that lived a long time ago.

 **Enemy**—somebody or something that tries to hurt another.

 **Extinct**—when a type of animal has died out.

Fierce—scary and dangerous.

 **Sail**—a big fin made of bones and covered in skin.

 **Signaling**—sending messages to other animals.

Index

Parents' and teachers' notes

- Look at the front cover. Ask your child what he or she thinks the book is about.
- Point out the title and the author's name. Explain that the "author" is the person who wrote the book.
- Look at the different parts of the book. Explain features such as the title page, the contents page, the main body of the book, the glossary, and the index. Explain the purpose of each of these parts.
- Ask if the book is fiction or nonfiction (i.e. if it is telling a story or giving information).
- Ask your child to look for the names of the dinosaurs. See if he or she can pronounce them. It does not matter if your child pronounces the names incorrectly—it is the exploration of the words that is important.
- Flick through the book. Discuss which pictures look the most exciting. Use this as an indication of which pages to read first. Explain that nonfiction books do not have to be read in order like a story.

- Has your child seen any other books about dinosaurs? Find examples and compare the illustrations of the animals. Explain that the pictures can be very different from one another because nobody has ever seen a real live dinosaur, so no one knows exactly what they looked like.
- Encourage your child to draw two or three pictures of an Ouranosaurus, in different colors. Which color scheme does your child think looks the best?
- Encourage your child to draw his or her own dinosaur landscape. Can he or she draw some plant-eating dinosaurs, eating from prehistoric trees? Can he or she draw a ferocious Tyrannosaurus rex?
- Ask your child to make up a story about what it would be like to live in the age of dinosaurs.
- Look back through the book and see if your child can remember the names of the dinosaurs. Discuss which dinosaur is his or her favorite and the reasons why.